THE ARK AND THE DARKNESS: UNEARTHING THE MYSTERIES OF NOAH'S FLOOD

STUDENT GUIDE

Elizabeth Isaacs
Edward Isaacs

Copyright © 2024 by Genesis Apologetics, Inc.
E-mail: staff@genesisapologetics.com

www.genesisapologetics.com
A 501(c)(3) ministry equipping youth pastors, parents, and students with the Biblical truth about Genesis, Creation, and the Flood.

The entire contents of this book (including videos) are available online: *www.noahsflood.com*

The Ark and the Darkness: Student Guide

by Elizabeth Isaacs & Edward Isaacs
Printed in the United States of America

ISBN: 9798323397563

All rights reserved solely by Genesis Apologetics. The author guarantees all contents are original and do not infringe upon the legal rights of any other person or work. No part of this book may be reproduced in any form without the permission of the author. The views expressed in this book are not necessarily those of the publisher.

Scripture taken from the The Holy Bible, English Standard Version® (ESV®) © 2001 by Crossway, a publishing ministry of Good News Publishers. ESV Text Edition: 2016

Download the FREE "Genesis Apologetics" Mobile App for Creation v. Evolution Videos!

Dedication

We would like to acknowledge Answers in Genesis (*www.answersingenesis.org*) and the Institute for Creation Research (*www.icr.org*). Much of the content herein has been drawn from (and is meant to be in alignment with) these Biblical Creation ministries.

"This is the Lord's doing; it is marvelous in our eyes."
—Psalm 118:23

Contents

About Genesis Apologetics 9
How to use this Study Guide 11
Session 1: The History 12
1.1: What has the world come to? 13
1.2: World in Freefall 14
1.3: Through the Looking-glass 19
1.4: Words of Wisdom 22
Session 2: The Judgement 25
2.1: Agents of Chaos 27
2.2: How It All Went Down 31
2.3: The Sediment Record 34
Session 3: The Monuments 37
3.1: Silent Witnesses 38
3.2: Dinosaur Soft Tissue 40
Session 4: The Fallout 43
4.1: On Hearts of Stone 44
4.2: The Way of Salvation 48
Fill in the Blank/Find it in Scripture Answer Key: 51
Helpful Resources 55
Prayer of Salvation 56

About Genesis Apologetics

Genesis Apologetics is a non-profit 501(c)(3) ministry that provides Christians with training programs for students of all ages covering Creation, Noah's Flood, the fossil record, gender sex and marriage, race, evolution, the reliability of the Bible, and others. Our programs have been used in schools around the world, translated into 13 languages, distributed by mainstream Christian outlets, and are available free online:

- *Noah's Flood Movie ("The Ark and the Darkness: Unearthing the Mysteries of Noah's Flood") and Resources: www.noahsflood.com*
- *Foundations Movie:* A free movie that shows just how important it is to believe in God's Word, starting with the very first page: *www.foundationsmovie.com*
- *Genesis Impact:* A free movie showing an equipped Christian debating a museum docent about the leading evidences for evolution in museums (great for preparing before visiting museums): *www.genesisimpact.com*
- *Mobile App:* Search *Genesis Apologetics* in App stores.
- *K-8 Students* enjoy our Student Zone: www.genesisapologetics.com/students.
- *5th-10th Graders* can learn from the **Debunking Evolution** program which takes apart the Top 10 pillars of evolution and contrasts them with the truth of Biblical Creation. Six video-based lessons and Student Guide workbook included! *www.debunkevolution.com*
- *11th-12th Graders* can use our **Debunking the Seven Myths** program to prepare for the Top Seven false teachings about Genesis, Creation, and Flood that they will encounter in college: *www.sevenmyths.com*
- YouTube Channel (**Genesis Apologetics**).
- Website: *www.genesisapologetics.com*

About the Authors

Elizabeth Isaacs is dedicated to sharing the truth found in God's Word from the very first verse. As a graduate student working on her Master of Education, she is focused on curriculum and instruction and enjoys working with students. Elizabeth holds a bachelor's degree centered in American Sign Language and Ministry, is passionate about keeping God at the center of everything, and helping students to be well-rounded and Biblically grounded.

With over a decade of study to his credit, *Edward A. Isaacs* is fascinated by the sciences and studying Earth history from the understanding that our Creator "has made His wonderful works to be remembered" (Psalms 111:4). A prolific writer, Edward has published dozens of technical articles on the geological processes of the Genesis Flood and ensuing Ice Age in peer-reviewed journals such as Journal of Creation and Creation Research Society Quarterly. As a creation researcher and educator, Edward serves as an ambassador of Logos Research Associates and research associate for Genesis Apologetics.

How to use this Study Guide

This Study Guide is meant to supplement the movie *The Ark and the Darkness: Unearthing the Mysteries of Noah's Flood*. The goal of the guide is to help digest and break down the information in the film, as well as give the opportunity for discussion or reflection.

While broken up into four main sessions, **we recommend taking your time and not rushing through the material or discussion questions**. If this means not getting through all the subsections for a session at once, simply start the following subsection the next time. It is not important to get completely through a session in one sitting.

Each session is estimated to be an hour in length, with 20-30 minutes of that being view time. There are 2-4 subsections in each session, each including the time stamps of the movie to watch, a fill in the blank section to complete while viewing, and discussion questions. ***It is important to pause the movie after each subsection.*** This allows processing time as the movie is very information dense and gives important time to discuss the topics while it is fresh in your brain!

Some subsections also have "Put it in Perspective" and/or "Digging Deeper" segments meant to enhance your understanding of the material. Finally, at the end of each session, there are vocabulary words and "Find it in Scripture!" sections. The Scripture segments are especially impactful as they will help you find and study the verses for yourself.
We hope this strengthens your faith and understanding of God's world!

—Elizabeth

Session 1: The History

Can you think back to a time when it went all wrong? Perhaps a time when carefully laid plans or, well, perhaps even poor ones somehow ended up in a less than pleasant situation? When such times happen, I tend to have my moments of "How could it come to this?" I sift through my memories, trying to uncover what led to the decisions or situations that brought on this disaster. Sometimes, in such cases, it is important to consider the steps that led us to where it all went wrong.

In our secular institutions, we see a culture that is saturated with the idea that "the present is the key to the past," that only the current course of nature is required to understand how our world has always operated. That idea in its modern form, however, is actually rather new, and the dangerous implications of that idea are still being discovered. Just as we do in the times we find ourselves in that unpleasant situation, we need to look into our *past* to better understand how we arrived at the present. In this first session, let us dive into our history to better understand our today.

1.1: What has the world come to?

"The Bible in fact tells us that the past is the key to the present and the Flood is key to understanding why the world is the way it is today." — Dr. Andrew Snelling

Watch: The Ark and the Darkness **0:00-7:42**, filling in the blanks as you go along.

Fill in the Blank:

1) Dr. Snelling: Conventional scientists, the secular scientists think that the present is the _____. The Bible tells us that the past is the _____ _____ and the _____ is key to understanding why the world is the way it is today.

2) Dr. Chaffey: When we look at the world around us, when we look at all of those hundreds and hundreds of rock layers, they're _____ layers, that means they were _____.

3) Dr. Haynes: He sent the Flood to punish evil at that time and that's _____ God sent the Flood. It's important to _____ evil. That's _____.

1.2: World in Freefall

"Creation was in a state of innocence. This affirms a fundamental element of God's character. He is good. God is not the author of evil or death." – Dr. John Sanford

Watch: The Ark and the Darkness **7:42-15:43**, filling in the blanks as you go along.

Fill in the Blank:

1) Dr. Price: _____, God saw everything that he had made and it was _____. It was just the way it should have been.

2) Dr. Sanford: Creation was in a state of innocence. This affirms a fundamental element of God's character. He is _____. God is not the author of _____ or _____.

3) Dr. Mortenson: The fall of man affected the _____ creation. The ground was _____.

4) Dr. Mortenson: We don't live in the original very good creation. We live in a _____ creation, a cursed creation. The fall was a massive, catastrophic _____ event.

Put it in Perspective (1.2): Death before sin?

We've all heard the evolutionary story that humans evolved from cells to fish to rodents to apes and then to humans. But is it true? Did God use evolution to create everything? Let's look a little closer at this idea—called theistic evolution—and death before sin.

Genesis 1:26 says, "Then God said, 'Let us make man in our image, after our likeness. And let them have dominion over the fish of the sea, and over the birds of the heavens and over the livestock and over all the earth and over every creeping things that creeps on the earth." God gave humans dominion over all the earth. God told them, "Be fruitful and multiply, fill the earth and subdue it ... I have given you every plant yielding seed ...and every tree with seed in its fruit. You shall have them for food. And to every beast of the earth and to every bird of the heavens and to everything that creeps on the earth, everything that has the breath of life, I have given every green plant for food" (Genesis 2:28-30).

This states that man is to have dominion over the earth and subdue it. In Genesis 2, God brings the animals to Adam to see what he would call them. The fact that humans were made in the image of God to have dominion over all the plants and animals sets us apart from the rest of Creation. Man is the crowning glory of God's Creation, to work it and to keep it. Secondly, the fact that all plants were given to both humans and animals (again note the distinction between them), means that everything was vegetarian at the beginning. There were no animals eating each other or chasing Adam and Eve. The Creation was very good according to the standards and character of God.

In Genesis 2, where God goes more in depth on how He created man, it states, "the Lord God formed the man from the dust of the ground and breathed into his nostrils the breath of life, and the man became a living creature" (Genesis 2:7). Here God again shows that He created man specially. For everything else, God spoke, and the light, land, plants, and animals came to being. Even the Creation of all the amazing stars in the universe were simply stated as an add on: "He made the stars also" (Genesis 1:16b). Yet with mankind, God specially formed man from the dust of the ground, and woman from the rib of a man. God specially formed man for a purpose, and then the man became a living creature. The Lord God took a rib from man's side and then made woman, specially and for a purpose. Finally, Jesus' own genealogy states "the son of Adam, the son of God" (Luke 3:38), linking Adam straight to God, without any "98% human" ancestors like evolutionists claim.

This picture of separate Creation for a purpose does not fit with the evolutionary theory, which states that man is the result of billions of years of death, disease, and mutations. In the fossil record, we see fossilized bones with cancer and diseases, broken bones, animals killing each other, and all sorts of thorns and thistles. According to evolution, death, animals eating animals, thorns and thistles all came before humans evolved.

But according to Genesis, Adam and Eve ate the fruit and sinned. Then God told Adam, *"Cursed is the ground because of you [...] thorns and thistles it shall bring forth for you [...] by the sweat of your face you shall eat bread, till you return to the ground..."* (Genesis 3:17-19). God says that death, disease, and thorns are a result of man's sin.

These two worldviews—Genesis 1-2 and evolution—are incompatible and don't match at all. Therefore, you are left with a choice- do you believe God's word or man's word? If you don't believe that Genesis 1-2 is God's word, then nothing from the last few paragraphs matters to you. After all, many people just take Genesis 1-2 out of the Bible anyways, right? Many people say that God could have used evolution. But wait—let's think about that for a minute. Do you believe in Jesus?

The Bible says that all Scripture is inspired by God (1 Timothy 3:16), and Jesus says, *"Have you not read that he who created them **from the beginning** made them male and female?"* (Luke 19:4). When Jesus tells the gospel message on the road to Emmaus, He started from the beginning! He did not simply say, "I came to save you from your sin." Instead, Jesus began from Moses and all the prophets, interpreting everything in Scripture about Himself (Luke 24:25-27). There are also many times when Jesus refers to Moses' writings (Genesis-Deuteronomy) as true and real history, saying, *"For if you believed Moses, you would believe me; for he wrote of me. But if you do not believe his writings, how will you believe my words?"* (John 5:46-47).

If these things are not true, then Jesus' honesty or His beliefs about earth history can be called into question. But Peter writes that *"He committed no sin, neither was deceit found in his mouth* (1 Peter 2:22). Further, *"we do not have a high priest who is unable to sympathize with our weaknesses, but one who in every respect has been tempted as we are, yet without sin"* (Hebrews 4:15).

Since God is a perfect, righteous judge, He must punish our sin, our wrongdoing. Yet He provided a way to save us in His love. He sent Jesus to become flesh, God in human form, going through temptation by the devil just as Adam was, yet never sinning. It is because Jesus took on human flesh and lived perfectly that He could die on the cross, taking the punishment for our sin upon Himself.

> "Therefore, as one trespass led to condemnation for all men, so one act of righteousness leads to justification and life for all men. For as by the one man's disobedience the many were made sinners, so by the one man's obedience the many will be made righteous (Romans 5:18-19).

If death was not the result of sin, then this creates a huge problem. The entire reason Jesus died for our sin is part of God's redemption plan. Jesus' divinity commands both truthfulness and complete knowledge about the past. Genesis is the foundation of the gospel, and if Genesis is not true from the very first verse, the foundation for the New Testament crumbles. It is vital to trust God's word from beginning to end, or the entire gospel falls apart.

For Discussion:

1. Does this change the way you think or live your life? If so, how?

2. How do these two worldviews—real Genesis 1-2 and evolution—impact those who believe them? What difference does it make in someone's life? (Hint: start with the purpose of mankind).

3. How are you applying this to your life? How should this knowledge impact your life? Is there someone you know who needs to hear this?

1.3: Through the Looking-glass

"If you were to graph the lifespans of all the men after the Flood, you don't see a linear line gradually sloping down, as you would likely see if the ages were made up, but instead, what you see is an exponentially decaying curve with minor variations since no two people are alike." – Narrator

Watch: The Ark and the Darkness **15:43-21:12**, filling in the blanks as you go along.

Fill in the Blanks:

1) Dr. Snelling: The amount of vegetation in the pre-flood world was far _____, far more _____.

2) Dr. Mortenson: We have many creatures in the fossil record that are just like today, but they were much _____, so _____ in the fossil record. That indicates that the pre-flood world was much more _____ for biological life.

3) Dr. Chaffey: Originally at least, it wouldn't have had _____ mountain ranges, it wouldn't have had huge _____ areas. God created the world to be _____.

4) Dr. Sanford: Adam and Eve had no _____. The first 10 patriarchs before the Flood had very low mutation rates, and so they were all living to be about the same age. Something happened at the time of the _____.

5) Narrator: The post-flood lifespans of the genealogical line of Adam follow a _____ concept known as _____.

Put it in Perspective (1.3): Mutations

In the beginning, God created everything perfectly, because He is perfect, and He said everything was *very good*. Adam and Eve were then created perfectly, without mutations. After the fall of man, they began to decay and mutations began. After the Flood, the mutation rate increased because there were only four couples coming off the ark as well as a changed environment. This "genetic bottleneck" would have made the lifespans go down quickly—but not in a straight line. The Bible records exactly what scientists would have expected after a global catastrophe—people decaying on a predictable mathematical exponential decay curve with minor variations.

For Discussion:

1. The scientists in the film discussed the pre-flood world being more lush and habitable with larger animals. Evolutionists have called this the pre-historic world. Given what we are told in Genesis, is this world truly "pre-historic" or simply a unique combination of creatures and environments that existed before the Flood?
2. After reading "Put it in Perspective 1.3," how has this impacted your thinking? How do you think this can affect others?

For Further Study: "What was the Pre-flood World Like?" and "How did People Live to be Over 900 Years Old Before the Flood?" from *The Ark and the Darkness* companion book.

1.4: Words of Wisdom

"I looked at the geometry of the cross-section and of the length of just the straightforward reading of the Bible, and I found out that it's dynamically stable, 90 degrees in pitch mode and 90 degrees in yaw mode, meaning it'll go all the up to 90 degrees and it'll come back. It's stable."
— Dr. Mark Horstemeyer

Watch: The Ark and the Darkness **21:12-30:07**, filling in the blanks as you go along.

Fill in the Blanks:

1) Dr. Horstemeyer: (The Ark) will go all the up to 90 degrees and it'll _____. It's _____.

2) Dr. Mortenson: The Bible doesn't say that Noah was to take two of every species onto the Ark, it was to take two of every _____.

3) Narrator: The sea creatures, insects, invertebrates, and plant species did _____ to be included on the ark.

4) Narrator: God instructed Noah to only bring the vertebrae land animals, and when you simplify those animals to their genealogical class structure found in Genesis, which is known as a _____, you can further significantly reduce the number of animals needed down to around roughly _____ kinds or approximately _____ animals in total.

5) Narrator: You also don't need to bring fully mature adults, when smaller juveniles would fit better, _____ less, waste less, and live _____ while reproducing in the post-flood world.

Put it in Perspective (1.4): What is a Kind?

One of the first questions people ask about Noah's Flood is "How do you fit all the animals in the ark?" There are millions of different types of animals in the world. God told Noah "*And of every living thing of all flesh, you shall bring two of every* **kind** *into the ark, to keep them alive with you; they shall be male and female*" (Genesis 6:19, NASB). What exactly is a *kind*?

Think about dogs—you have Great Danes, German Shepherds, Chihuahuas, Corgis, Golden Retrievers, and so many more! Yet they are all dogs. People have bred them over the years to refine certain character traits so that the different breeds appear uniquely different, yet they can still all interbreed because they all share a common genetic and parental history. Noah would have taken two dogs that had all the genetic variation required to create the many breeds today.

For Further Study: "How Could the Ark Have Been Seaworthy?" and "How Could All the Animals Fit on the Ark?" from *The Ark and the Darkness* companion book.

Session 1: Find it in Scripture!
Match the statements to the Bible verse that most closely matches it:

A. Psalm 34:8
B. Genesis 1:11-25
C. 1 Cor. 15:21-22
D. Romans 5:12
E. Genesis 5:1-32
F. Genesis 11:10-32
G. Romans 8:19-25
H. Titus 3:4-8

_____ 1. "We live in a fallen creation, a cursed creation."
_____ 2. "The first 10 patriarchs were living to be about the same age." – Dr. Sanford
_____ 3. The genealogy follows an exponential decay curve.
_____ 4. Out of love, Jesus died for our sin.
_____ 5. "This affirms a fundamental element of God's character. He is good." – Dr. Sanford
_____ 6. Death is the result of man's sin.
_____ 7. The second Adam has reversed the effects of the first Adam.
_____ 8. A kind is God's classification system meaning animals and plants that reproduce together.

Below are some of the verses outside of Genesis that talk about Adam. Think about how these verses (and the ones mentioned in Section 1.2) would affect your faith if Adam was not a real person specially created by God. Be sure to read the verses in their context.

1 Cor. 15:47   Hosea 6:7   Matthew 19:4   Acts 17:26
2 Cor. 11:3   1 Timothy 2:13

Session 2: The Judgement

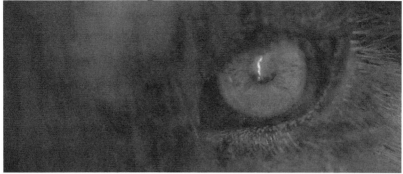

The Flood was a divine judgement, a cataclysm sent to judge humanity for the dark path it had embarked on. It was a unique event, with no predecessor and never to be repeated (see Genesis 9:12-16). This was a limited-edition geologic event that impacted the world on a global scale. Shouldn't there be some signs of that event? Some way we can look out at our world to better understand what happened?

Fortunately for us, the account of the Flood was recorded in Genesis 7 and 8, giving us a starting point for piecing together the story in a way much like how a criminal investigator might piece together the clues from witnesses in a murder mystery. As in the case of the murder mystery, what we are told in Genesis has limitations. Most of what we are told in Genesis is from the perspective of Noah. He could see when the rain started, the waves rose, and how the world that he knew was swallowed up into chaos, but he had no way of knowing what was happening everywhere at any time. He couldn't, for instance, know what was happening deep underground.

Genesis gives us a starting place to begin our investigation, but it doesn't give us the entire picture. To fill in the details, we must search for clues ourselves to put together the pieces. Those many scattered clues are then put together into "Flood models," which are storylines of how the Flood might have begun and unwound for its year-long lifespan. It is important to keep in mind that these Flood models are *representations* of how the Flood could have occurred. Yes, we have the general account in Genesis which we can have full confidence, but beyond that we are guaranteed nothing. Despite our best efforts, we can never understand the full picture. We can try to make sense of it all, but we can never fully understand exactly how it happened.

Think about it this way: imagine a friend who, for whatever reason, can't seem to get along with you. You observe their behavior and do your best to understand why it is that they brush you off so quickly or go out of their way to put you down. You imagine to yourself why it is they act this way, but, unless they honestly tell you why, you can never truly know why they act the way that they do. The reasons for their actions can be many, and although we can sometimes have a general idea why, we can never truly understand them.

Flood models are similar. We can observe the data in the same way that we can observe the person, and we can come up with these grand explanations for how the Flood occurred or why it is this person acts that way, but the true reason will always remain a mystery to some degree or other. Flood models are potential explanations for how the Flood might have happened, but until we can talk to the Orchestrator of that judgement, our grandest models are still only our best guesses. Though this movie decided to show the Flood occurring as suggested by an idea called Catastrophic Plate Tectonics, it is important to remember that this is just one possible way the Flood could have occurred. Every Flood model has its weak points, and that is why scientists will have to continue searching for clues for years to come to get a better idea of what happened during the Flood. Perhaps you will be one of those scientists who helps people understand how terrible yet magnificent this divine judgement truly was.

2.1: Agents of Chaos

"The purpose of the Flood, contrary to what many think, it was not simply to destroy sinful man, but also Genesis 6 tells this, "To destroy all the land, animals, and birds not in the ark with Noah and to destroy the surface of the earth," and only a global flood would accomplish that purpose."
– Dr. Terry Mortenson

The global nature of the Flood is clearly explained in the biblical text through its specific use of key words and phrases. The term for the Flood itself is *mabbul*, which is a unique Hebrew word. This word makes an appearance in only one other place in the Old Testament, specifically in Psalm 29:10 where it says that God sat as king at the Flood. Indeed, it is a uniquely distinct term that sets this Flood event apart from other types of floods recorded in scripture. Consider some of the language used in Genesis:

> *Everything* that is under the *whole* heaven, under the *whole* earth, *everything* in which is the breath of life (Genesis 6:17).

Notice the use of words like "all" and "every" and even universal terms such as "under the whole heaven." The importance of these phrases is made all the more clear through the repetition of those words, which in the original language was like making text italics or bold to draw attention to something important.

Why was it so important that the reader understand the Flood's global nature? The purpose of the Flood, as introduced previously, was not simply to destroy sinful man. Instead, Genesis 6 tells us that the Flood was, "To destroy all the land, animals, and birds not in the ark with Noah and to destroy the surface of the earth." Such a mission could only be accomplished by a global flood. Incidentally, the Genesis Flood lasted 370 days. Local floods may last a few days or perhaps even a few weeks, but over a year? Only something of such massive proportions like that of a global could have lasted so long. Just think about it: there is no way a local flood could last that long. It even covered all the high mountains everywhere under the heavens.

To take it another step further, there is the matter of an ark, intended to, "keep offspring alive on the face of all the earth," as Genesis 7:3 says. Its purpose was to preserve humanity and representatives of air-breathing land animals, yet, if the flood was only local, there would be no need to build an ark. Noah and his family could have strolled to some exotic vacation resort in a safer part of the world. Animals too could migrate as necessary, and birds would simply have to stay above the fray during the Flood. Instead, we see that God specifically commands Noah to design the things necessary to withstand a flood of global proportions.

Finally, there is a theological concept at stake here because the second coming is directly compared to the Flood. If during the Flood there were men elsewhere who were not part of the judgment of the Flood, then the whole idea of a judgment on mankind for corruption of the earth would make no sense whatsoever. God says, "I've seen the wickedness of man that's great on the earth," not just in one local place but on the earth. When we come to the New Testament, you have a passage like 2 Peter 3:5-7, which compares a flood that destroyed the world with a future judgment that would one day destroy the world. If you had a local judgment in the past, you'd have to have a local judgment in the future, but of course, this is the second coming of Jesus Christ to judge His world, and it has to be universal.

Watch: The Ark and the Darkness **30:07-34:30**, filling in the blanks as you go along.

Fill in the Blanks:

1) Dr. Mortenson: The unique Hebrew word, *mabbul*, it's used _____ _____ other place in the Old Testament. That is in Psalm 29:10 where it says that God sat as king at the Flood.

2) Dr. Price: It's a very _____ term that sets this account apart from other types of floods.

3) Dr. Mortenson: "To destroy _____ the land, animals, and birds not in the ark with Noah and to destroy the surface of the earth," and only a _____ Flood would accomplish that purpose.

5) Dr. Price: When the scripture says that the waters rose to about 24 feet _____ the mountains, even if you give the idea that the mountains were not as high as they are now...you still have water only rising to its _____.

5) Dr. Price: You also have the very theological concept that if you had men elsewhere who were not part of the judgment of the Flood, then the whole idea of a judgment on _____ for corruption of the earth would make no sense whatsoever.

29

For Discussion:

1. Although the Bible is full of history and poetry, it is possible for many of its passages to have multiple meanings that provide a more complete picture of what is being displayed, with many of these secondary meanings being more symbolic in nature. In that light, what symbols do you think God used to communicate through with the construction of the Ark?
2. In Genesis 9, God makes a promise to never destroy the earth with a flood again, making the rainbow the symbol of this promise. Why is that important when considering the suggestion that Noah's Flood could have been local?

For further study: "Was Noah's Flood Only Local? Not Even a Chance" and "When was Noah's Flood and How Long did it Last?" from *The Ark and the Darkness* companion book.

2.2: How It All Went Down

"It's no accident that there's an order given there in the scriptures. The fountains of the deep broke open, that is the crust breaking open, the water shooting up, the supersonic steam jets, and carrying that ocean water up. Then, it fell as global torrential rainfall."
– Dr. Andrew Snelling

Watch: The Ark and the Darkness **34:30-46:42**, filling in the blanks as you go along.

Fill in the Blanks:

1) Dr. Snelling: It's no accident that there's an order given there in the scriptures. The fountains of the deep broke open, that is the _____ breaking open, the water shooting up, the supersonic _____ jets and carrying that ocean water up. Then, it fell as global torrential _____.

2) Narrator: A man named Abraham Ortelius, a famous cartographer from the _____, first proposed the idea that the Flood of Noah may have been responsible for tearing apart the Americas from _____ and Africa.

3) Narrator: Hundreds of years later, another Christian by the name of Antonio Snider-Pellegrini would first theorize the

modern concept of _____ in which he illustrated two maps depicting the continents of the world as once joined together.

4) Narrator: In the _____, technology initially developed to detect submarines underwater stumbled across these gigantic scars from the fountains of the great deep that had split open exactly as the _____ had described.

5) Narrator: Scientists will later discover that the seafloor at the Mid-Atlantic Ridge is much _____ than the seafloor in other parts of the world exactly as the Bible suggests. As this newly emerging volcanic floor spreads, it _____ under the west coast of North America, binding and releasing, causing massive tsunamis.

For Discussion:

1. How can better understanding the inner workings of the Flood impact our daily lives? Is it simply an interesting hobby for some people, or does it have practical applications such as in the real world or in apologetics?
2. How would you distinguish between a flood model and the historical account in Genesis? Why is it important to understand the differences, and what should our confidence be in either of them?

For further study: "How it all Happened: Catastrophic Plate Tectonics" from *The Ark and the Darkness* companion book.

Digging Deeper: Mars: Compared to Earth, Mars is a desert planet of drifting sand near its equator and chilling ice caps near its poles. It has been a shocking discovery then to find out that Mars likely had a very watery past. Since the 1980s, pictures taken of Mars using artificial satellites have revealed many features consistent with a water past. Giant canyons that cut across Mars surface are on a scale that dwarfs anything modern floods have created on Earth. Many scientists now believe that Mars once had an ocean that *covered nearly a third* of the planet's surface. Around this ocean were many lakes that, in some cases, flooded the landscape as "megafloods." This realization comes after years of rejection by scientists who claimed that such floods were impossible and that their very mention should be shunned because they seemed too "biblical" in proportion. As time goes on, however, scientists continue to learn how flooding has formed an important part of these planets' geologic history. What more will we learn in the years to come, and how might that shed light on Earth's greatest flood of all time?

2.3: The Sediment Record

"The most compelling evidence for a global flood is the sediment record itself. All over the earth, what's under your feet, hundreds of distinct horizontal layers generally with smooth interfaces between the layers. The only way that such a record could have come into existence is global scale processes producing the whole record in a single global event."
—Dr. John Baumgardner

Watch: The Ark and the Darkness **46:42-57:23**, filling in the blanks as you go along.

Fill in the Blanks:

1) Dr. Werner: The tsunamis then originating from the ocean areas would then race across the continents. Once the tsunami lost its _____, the sediment would _____ down out of the water and form a _____ _____ at the bottom.

2) Narrator: Given that the earth's surface is made up mostly of water formed _____ rock layers, the fact that the layers were actually formed in water also explains

why there is no _____ found in between the layers as there would be if the layers took millions of years to form.

3) Narrator: Bent and folded rock could only occur if the layers were pliable and _____ at the time of the bending. The bent layers also prove that their formation was _____ with multiple layers forming rapidly on top of each other because the bottom layers would still have to be saturated with _____.

4) Narrator: It's impossible for trees to remain intact for millions of years while layers of dirt and debris slowly piled around them and rain and moisture rot the wood out. Instead, [...] tsunami waves would carry in sediments that would _____ the trees quickly in _____ layers.

5) Narrator: Geologists discovered that the same sand from the _____ _____ of America had been carried in tsunami waves all the way to the _____ _____ of the continent.

For Discussion:

1. What forms of erosion do you see in our world today? Do you think that it is possible for completely flat layers to exist without erosion over millions of years? Support your answer.
2. Think about trying to bend a rock. What happens? If it doesn't bend naturally, what circumstances would help the rock bend? (Hint: think about the differences of soft clay, hardened clay, and baked clay).
3. When you walk outside and look at dead trees, what do you see? Are trees becoming hard like rocks? Evolutionists often claim that the present is the key to the past. Is what you observe with dead trees consistent

with the theory that each rock layer around a tree took millions of years? Why or why not?

For further study: "How it all Happened: Catastrophic Plate Tectonics" from *The Ark and the Darkness* companion book.

Session 2: Find it in Scripture!

Read Genesis 7:6-8:22 and letter them A-H by the order found in Scripture:

_____ 1. The rain fell for 40 days and 40 nights.
_____ 2. The water prevailed upon the earth for 150 days.
_____ 3. The waters of the Flood rose about 24 feet above the mountains.
_____ 4. 10 months from the start of the Flood, the top of the mountains became visible.
_____ 5. The fountains of the deep and the floodgates of heaven were closed, and the rain stopped.
_____ 6. 13 months after the Flood started, the land was dry and God told Noah and his family to get off the ark.
_____ 7. The Lord blotted out all land animals, birds, and people from the earth except those on the ark.
_____ 8. The fountains of the great deep burst open.

Read through Genesis 6 and 7. How many times can you count the words "all," "every," "under heaven," "the whole earth," and other such universal phrases?

Session 3: The Monuments

Every great disaster leaves its mark on the landscape. Just imagine any flood or wildfire—debris strewn across the plain, wreckage of a dozen homes crumpled together, or the scorched ground that blackens the hills. These events can leave marks of their coming and going for years to come. Would it not make sense then that something as great as a global flood would leave behind some record of its passing? Not just any record, but one of the most remarkable ever to be read?

As it turns out, when we look across our world, we have many such "silent witnesses" in the form of fossils that testify to a global flood. Some may like to say that "the devil is in the details," but the deeper we look into the cases of these silent witnesses, the more remarkable their story truly becomes!

3.1: Silent Witnesses

"To produce a fossil, in most cases, especially for the larger kinds of organisms, requires complete burial and rapid burial, and that automatically speaks of catastrophic conditions. So the fact that we find so many fossils, so well preserved, many of them with evidence that the animals were buried alive, is another powerful evidence for a flood cataclysm."
—Dr. John Baumgardner

Watch: The Ark and the Darkness **57:23-1:08:07**, filling in the blanks as you go along.

Fill in the Blanks:

1) Dr. Baumgardner: To produce a fossil, in most cases, especially for the larger kinds of organisms, requires _____ and _____ burial, and that automatically speaks of catastrophic conditions.

2) Dr. Snelling: The fossils have been exquisitely preserved. […] For example, a fish about to _____ another fish, and it's been buried. That tells you it had to be very _____ to preserve those details.

3) Dr. Werner: All of the rock layers of the world, the named rock layers like the Cambrian, the Jurassic, _____ of the layers of the world have _____ creatures […] in the _____ of the continents.

4) Narrator: You are essentially given two choices today. On the one hand, you have a book written thousands of years ago giving an amazingly detailed account of a worldwide flood that wiped out virtually all life on earth. On the other hand, you have _____ theories, in this case, one that was only first postulated about 40 years ago due to the _____ of their prior non-catastrophic models that they know really didn't work.

For Discussion:

1. What fossils have you seen that are in "life" positions that require instant burial?
2. Of the sedimentary and fossil evidence you have heard (fossils in life positions, sea creatures in the middle of continents and on mountains, the same rock layer stretching across the continent, etc.), which do you think makes the best case for a global flood and why?

For further study: "Why an Asteroid Did Not Wipe Out the Dinosaurs" from *The Ark and the Darkness* companion book.

3.2: Dinosaur Soft Tissue

"We started looking inside of this bone, and we found, using scanning electron microscopy, that it had elastic material. It had tissue. You pull it apart, and it goes back. If this was mineralized or it was a fossil that became a rock, you couldn't do this. So it was never mineralized, never petrified. It was still elastic, which means it was still the tissue. That means this thing is not 100 million years old." – Dr. Mark Horstemeyer

Watch: The Ark and the Darkness **1:08:07-1:18:48**, filling in the blanks as you go along.

Fill in the Blanks:

1) Dr. Horstemeyer: Mary Schweitzer in the _____ and the early 2000s first found this _____ material in arteries (of a T-rex femur). Elastic material means you pull it, and it reloads back to its original place.

2) Dr. Horstemeyer: If this (elastic material) was mineralized or was a _____, …you couldn't do this. So it was never mineralized, never petrified. It was still elastic, which means it was still the _____. That means this thing is not 100 million years old.

3) Narrator: Collagen doesn't even last _____ as long as it would have to in order for evolution theory to work.

4) Narrator: Dinosaur graveyards like these would later be found _____ _____ the earth, and secular paleontologists agree that these worldwide sites share one thing in common, the state the bones are found in all show evidence of _____ burial.

For Discussion:

1. Bio-organic material doesn't last very long even when best preserved, yet scientists have discovered over 16 types of soft tissue in dinosaur bones. What impact does this have on both creation and evolution?
2. The word 'dinosaur' was not coined until 1841 after most English translations had become standard, but that doesn't mean that creatures like dinosaurs are excluded from Scripture. As you go through the "Find it in Scripture" below, think about what sort of creature God is describing to Job.

For further study: "Dinosaur Fossils: Look No Further if you Want Evidence for the Worldwide Flood," "Noah's Flood: How did People and Animals Disperse Around the World after the Flood?" and "Dinosaurs after the Flood—there be Dragons!" from *The Ark and the Darkness* companion book.

Session 3: Find it in Scripture!

A. Genesis 40:15
B. Genesis 40:16
C. Genesis 40:17
D. Genesis 40:18
E. Genesis 40:19

_____ 1. Chief of the ways of God
_____ 2. Sinews of its thighs are close knit
_____ 3. Strength in its loins
_____ 4. Sways its tail like a cedar tree
_____ 5. Bones tubes of bronze
_____ 6. Power in the muscles of its belly
_____ 7. Eats grass like an ox
_____ 8. Limbs like rods of iron

See the YouTube video titled, "Does the Bible (Job 40) Describe a Sauropod Dinosaur (Behemoth) (ver.2)?" for more about dinosaurs and the Bible.

Session 4: The Fallout

It is at this point we find ourselves at the cross-roads of some great history book and a high fantasy novel. After a time of desperation, the great battle has been waged and won. The conflict is now ended and the enemy nowhere to be found. Meanwhile, the heroes have been rescued and the world has finally been put back on the right track. Unlike those fantastical adventures of lands far away, however, this tale does not end here. In fact, the climax to this epic saga would not come until much, much later. At this juncture, evil survives yet to corrupt the hearts of humanity, but even in its corruption it cannot destroy the memory of a judgement—a judgement that came with a promise that would one day free the world for good.

4.1: On Hearts of Stone

"From Genesis 12 onward, we don't see similarities anymore. There's no Abraham legend. There's no Isaac legend, David Legend, or anything like that. But Genesis 1 through 11, people all around the globe seem to know about. Why? Because what the Bible's telling us is true, and up until Genesis 11 at the Babel event, mankind had a shared history, and then they took that history with them." – Dr. Tim Chaffey

Psalm 111:4 states that God "has made His wonderful works to be remembered." As one of God's supreme acts of judgment, the Flood has been instilled into the memories of the peoples of the world. Documented by anthropologists, missionaries, and others, about 200 flood traditions can be found across the world, including from groups that do not live anyway close to the ocean. In many of these cases, there are striking similarities to the biblical account. A righteous family is saved from a flood sent as judgement from the god(s) due to something that humanity had done to anger the god(s). These legends go on to talk about man and animals surviving on some kind of a boat.

The fascinating element of this story is that, in terms of how ideas progress, we know that history can become more mythical. Myth, as a core idea, cannot become more historical. It doesn't go the other way. History could become more historical. Myth becomes more mythical, and if you start with myth, you end up with myth. You can never go the other way.

As such, you would expect the historically accurate account of a global flood to be represented by the most historical-style narrative.

Consider the shape of the ark. The Babylonian Gilgamesh Epic has a cube for the ark, which would continually roll in the water until long after everything on board would die. In like manner, the Gilgamesh Epic speaks of a flood only six days long. It only took one week to build this huge ark. In comparison, the Bible describes the global Flood transpiring over the course of 371 days after is likely took Noah some 55 years or so to construct his ark.

The biblical account is the true account, and these other stories are the result of people migrating from the Tower of Babel after the Flood and preserving in their memory an echo of the true account that is recorded in Genesis. The farther they moved away from the Middle East and any contact with the true account, the more the story got corrupted over time. So that explains the differences as well as the similarities.

Watch: The Ark and the Darkness **1:18:48-1:29:11**, filling in the blanks as you go along.

Fill in the Blanks:

1) Dr. Price: We know that history can become more _____. Myth, as a core idea, _____ become more historical. […] Myth becomes more mythical, and if you start with myth, you end up with _____. You can never go the other way.

2) Dr. Chaffey: There are hundreds of flood legends from around the world, but in many of these cases, you have huge _____ to the biblical account. You have one

righteous family that is saved, and the reason for the Flood is because God was angry.

3) Dr. Mortenson: The farther they moved away from the Middle East and any contact with the _____ account, the more the story got _____ over time. So that explains the differences as well as the similarities.

4) Dr. Chaffey: From Genesis 12 onward, we _____ see similarities anymore. There's no Abraham legend. There's no Isaac legend, David Legend, or anything like that. But Genesis 1 through 11, people all around the _____ seem to know about.

5) Dr. Mortenson: People then, who were biologically, genetically very close, began to marry within their language group. From what we know of genetics, that would bring out recessive genes to become _____ and physical characteristics associated with that. But the Bible's very clear. There's only _____ race, Adam's race.

6) Narrator: Many of the earliest languages _____ to one location on earth, a place commonly referred to as the cradle of civilization, _____. And what's also revealing is that the timeframe of many languages also trace back to that approximate point in time, which is just after the Flood and Tower of Babel.

For Discussion:

1. Think of some myths or legends that you know (For example: Paul Bunyan, Johnny Appleseed, Washington/Jefferson/Lincoln and the cherry tree) and then discuss the following questions:

      a. Of these legends, do you think they started as history?
      b. If so, how did they become legends?
      c. Can these legends become history? Why or why not?
2. How does a scriptural understanding of history help us counteract racism or prejudice against other peoples?

For further study: "Flood Legends from Around the World" from *The Ark and the Darkness* companion book.

4.2: The Way of Salvation

"We've heard that the Ark of Noah was an ark constructed for the salvation of mankind. It had one door in it, and that was a single entrance. That was done by design. God also only has one way of salvation." – Dr. Randall Price

Watch: The Ark and the Darkness **1:29:11-END**, filling in the blanks as you go along.

Fill in the Blanks:

1) Dr. Price: When we come to the story of Noah's Ark, it's more than just a story. It certainly is a part of vital history. There was an ancient world. And that ancient world, because of _____, was destroyed by a _____. And that was the judgment. It was all mankind. Since man is not changed, there is yet a future judgment coming.

2) Dr. Mortenson: And Jesus says just before He returns, people will be in _____, ignoring _____, just going on living their life as if _____ doesn't exist. They will be _____ when Jesus comes and brings judgment.

3) Dr. Price: There was a judgment that happened and there's a judgment that is coming. We need to be _____.

For Discussion:

1. How does better understanding the Flood (that is, our past) help us better understand the final judgment (our future)? What lessons can we take from the Flood as we look forward to the second coming?
2. How do you think it would have been like to have been Noah? What sort of challenges do you think he and his family had to face, and how would those be similar to or differ from the challenges we as Christians face today? In your answer, consider questions such as:
    a. Would Noah have been mocked or accepted by society for his faith in God?
    b. Do Noah's actions illustrate his faith in God or in the society?
    c. Did Noah try to share with others the way of rescue or did he keep the good news hidden?
    d. In James 2:26, we are told that "faith without works is dead." What does this mean, and how does Noah illustrate this? (Ephesians 2:8-9)
3. Read John 15:18-21. How should this passage affect how you live your life?

For further study: "Dinosaur Fossils: Look No Further if you Want Evidence for the Worldwide Flood," "Noah's Flood: How did People and Animals Disperse Around the World after the Flood?" and "Dinosaurs after the Flood—there be Dragons!" from *The Ark and the Darkness* companion book.

Session 4: Find it in Scripture!

Match the statements to the Bible verse that most closely matches it:

A. 2 Peter 3:3-7
B. Genesis 9:11-17
C. Luke 17:24-27
D. Acts 17:26
E. John 3:16-18
F. Hebrews 11:7
G. John 14:6
H. Genesis 11:5-9

_____ 1. God confused the people's languages and scattered them across the earth.
_____ 2. Noah was righteous by faith.
_____ 3. Just as there was one door to the ark, so Jesus is the only way.
_____ 4. Scoffers will deliberately overlook the fact that the earth was globally flooded.
_____ 5. The rainbow is God's promise never to globally flood the earth again.
_____ 6. God sent His Son to take the punishment for our wrong, dying in our place, that we may have eternal life.
_____ 7. There is only one race.
_____ 8. The Flood has parallels to the end times.

Fill in the Blank/Find it in Scripture Answer Key:

Session 1.1:
1) Dr. Snelling: ...the present is the **key to the past**. ...the past is the **key to the present** and the **Flood** is key to understanding...
2) Dr. Chaffey: ...they're **sedimentary** layers, that means they were **laid down by water**.
3) Dr. Haynes: ...that's **why** God sent the Flood. It's important to **punish** evil. That's **justice**.

Session 1.2:
1) Dr. Price: **Before the fall**, God saw everything that he had made and it was **very good**. ...
2) Dr. Sanford: ... He is **good**. God is not the author of **evil** or **death**.
3) Dr. Mortenson: The fall of man affected the **whole** creation. The ground was **cursed**.
4) Dr. Mortenson: ... we live in a **fallen** creation, a cursed creation. The fall was a massive, catastrophic **world-changing** event.

Session 1.3:
1) Dr. Snelling: ... the pre-flood world was far **superior**, far more **luxuriant**.
2) Dr. Mortenson: ...they were much **larger**, so **giantism** in the fossil record. That indicates that the pre-flood world was much more **suitable** for biological life.
3) Dr. Chaffey: Originally at least, it wouldn't have had **impassable** mountain ranges, it wouldn't have had huge **desert** areas. God created the world to be **inhabited**.
4) Dr. Sanford: Adam and Eve had no **mutations**. ...at the time of the **Flood**.
5) Narrator: ...follow a **mathematical** concept known as **exponential decay**.

Session 1.4:
1) Dr. Horstemeyer: (The Ark) will go all the up to 90 degrees and it'll **come back**. It's **stable**.
2) Dr. Mortenson: …it was to take two of every **kind**.
3) Narrator: …did **not need** to be included on the ark.
4) Narrator: …is known as a **kind**, … roughly **1,400** kinds or approximately **6,750** animals…
5) Narrator: …juveniles would fit better, **eat** less, waste less, and live **longer** …

Session 1: Find it in Scripture:
1. G   2. E   3. B   4. H   5. A   6. D   7. C   8. B

Session 2.1:
1) Dr. Mortenson: The unique Hebrew word, mabbul, it's used **only one** other place…
2) Dr. Price: It's a very **unique** term that sets this account apart from other types of flood.
3) Dr. Mortenson: "To destroy **all** the land, animals, and birds…only a **global** flood…
4) Dr. Price: …24 feet **above** the mountains, …water only rising to its **own level**.
5) Dr. Price: …the whole idea of a judgment on **mankind** for corruption of the earth…

Session 2.2:
1) Dr. Snelling: …the **crust** breaking…the supersonic **steam** jets…global torrential **rainfall**.
2) Narrator: …cartographer from the **1500s**, …tearing apart the Americas from **Europe**…
3) Narrator: …first theorize the modern concept of **continental drift**…
4) Narrator: In the **1950s**, …split open exactly as the **Bible** had described.
5) Narrator: …Mid-Atlantic Ridge is much **younger** than the seafloor …volcanic floor spreads, it **subducts** under the west coast of North America…

Session 2.3:
1) Dr. Werner: … tsunami lost its **power**, the sediment would **settle** down out of the water and form a **flat layer** at the bottom.
2) Narrator: …water-formed **sedimentary** rock …no **erosion** found in between the layers…
3) Narrator: …if the layers were pliable and **soft** at the time of the bending, …their formation was **rapid** with multiple layers … with **water** and didn't have enough time to dry out.
4) Narrator: …what the **evidence** shows is …**bury** the trees quickly in **multiple** layers.
5) Narrator: Geologists discovered that the same sand from the **eastern side** of America had been carried in tsunami waves all the way to the **west side** of the continent.

Session 2: Find it in Scripture:
1.B   2. E   3. C   4. G   5. F   6. H   7. D   8. A

Session 3.1:
1) Dr. Baumgardner: …requires **complete** and **rapid** burial…
2) Dr. Snelling: …a fish about to **swallow** another fish, and it's been buried. That tells you it had to be very **rapid** to preserve those details.
3) Dr. Werner: …**all** of the layers…have **saltwater** creatures…in the **middle** of the continent.
4) Narrator: …you have **manmade** theories, …due to the **inadequacy** of their prior…

Session 3.2:
1) Dr. Horstemeyer: Mary Schweitzer in the **1990s** …first found this **elastic** material…
2) Dr. Horstemeyer: If this (elastic material) was mineralized or was a **fossil**, …it was still elastic, which means it was still the **tissue**.
3) Narrator: Collagen doesn't even last **0.001%** as long as it would have to…
4) Narrator: Dinosaur graveyards like these would later be found **all over** the earth…all show evidence of **flood** burial.

Session 3: Find it in Scripture:
1. E   2. C   3. B   4. C   5. D   6. B   7. A   8. D

Session 4.1:
1) Dr. Price: We know that history can become more **mythical**. Myth, as a core idea, **cannot** become more historical. …you start with myth, you end up with **myth**.
2) Dr. Chaffey: …Flood legends from around the world…have huge **similarities** to the biblical account.
3) Dr. Mortenson: The farther they moved away from …the **true** account, the more the story got **corrupted** over time…
4) Dr. Chaffey: From Genesis 12 onward, we **don't** see similarities…But Genesis 1 through 11, people all around the **globe** seem to know about.
5) Dr. Mortenson: …recessive genes to become **dominant** …There's only **one** race…
6) Narrator: Many of the earliest languages **trace back** to one location on earth, a place commonly referred to as the cradle of civilization, **Mesopotamia**. …

Session 4.2:
1) Dr. Price: … ancient world, because of **corruption**, was destroyed by a **flood**. …
2) Dr. Mortenson: …people will be in **rebellion**, ignoring **God**, just going on living their life as if **God** doesn't exist. They will be **surprised** when Jesus comes and brings judgment.
3) Dr. Price: …We need to be **prepared**.

Session 4: Find it in Scripture:
1. H   2. F   3. G   4. A   5. B   6. E   7. D   8. C

Helpful Resources

Genesis Apologetics

Mobile App:
Search for the free "Genesis Apologetics" App in the iTunes or Google Play stores.

Free Books and Videos:
5th–10th Grade Students: *www.debunkevolution.com*
11th grade-College: *www.sevenmyths.com*

YouTube Channel:
Channel Name: Genesis Apologetics

Dinosaurs:
www.genesisapologetics.com/dinosaurs

Theistic Evolution
www.genesisapologetics.com/theistic

"Lucy" (leading human evolution icon):
www.genesisapologetics.com/lucy

Answers in Genesis
www.answersingenesis.org

Institute for Creation Research
www.icr.org

Creation Ministries International
www.creation.com

Evolution: The Grand Experiment
www.thegrandexperiment.com

Creation Website Search Tool
www.searchcreation.org

Prayer of Salvation

You're not here by accident—God *loves* you and He *knows* who you are like no one else. His Word says:

> Lord, You have searched me and known me. You know my sitting down and my rising up; you understand my thought afar off. You comprehend my path and my lying down, and are acquainted with all my ways. For there is not a word on my tongue, but behold, O Lord, You know it altogether. You have hedged me behind and before, and laid Your hand upon me. Such knowledge is too wonderful for me; It is high, I cannot attain it. (Psalm 139:1–6)

God loves you with an everlasting love, and with a love that can cover all of your transgressions—all that you have ever done wrong. But you have to repent of those sins and trust the Lord Jesus Christ for forgiveness. Your past is in the past. He wants to give you a new future and new hope.

But starting this new journey requires a step—a step of faith. God has already reached out to you as far as He can. By giving His Son to die for your sins on the Cross, He's done everything He can to reach out to you. The next step is yours to take, and this step requires faith to receive His Son, Jesus, into your heart. It also requires repentance (turning away) from sin–a surrendered heart that is willing to reject a sinful lifestyle. Many believers have a much easier time leaving sinful lifestyles after they fully trust Jesus and nobody else and nothing else. Along with forgiveness, the Holy Spirit enters your life when you receive Jesus, and He will lead you into a different lifestyle and way—a way that will lead to blessing, joy, patient endurance under trials, and eternal life with Him.

If you are ready to receive Him, then consider four key Biblical truths.

1. Acknowledge that your sin separates you from God. Most simply, sin is our failure to measure up to God's holiness and His righteous standards. We sin by things we do, choices we make, attitudes we show, and thoughts we entertain. We also sin when we fail to do right things or even think right thoughts. The Bible also says that all people are sinners: "there is none righteous, not even one." No matter how good we try to be, none of us does right things all the time. The Bible is clear, "For all have sinned and come short of the glory of God" (Romans 3:23). Admit it. Agree with God on this one.
2. Our sins demand punishment—the punishment of death and separation from God. However, because of His great love, God sent His only Son Jesus to die for our sins: "God demonstrates His own love for us in this: While we were still sinners, Christ died for us" (Romans 5:8). For you to come to God, you have to get rid of your sin problem. But, in our own strength, not one of us can do this! You can't make yourself right with God by being a better person. Only God can rescue us from our sins. He is willing to do this, not because of anything you can offer Him, but **just because He loves you!** "He saved us, not because of righteous things we had done, but because of His mercy" (Titus 3:5).
3. It's only God's grace that allows you to come to Him—not your efforts to "clean up your life" or work your way to Heaven. You can't earn it. It's a free gift: "For it is by grace you have been saved, through faith—and this not from yourselves, it is the gift of God—not by works, so that no one can boast" (Ephesians 2:8–9). Will you accept this gift?
4. For you to come to God, the penalty for your sin must be paid. God's gift to you is His son, Jesus, who paid the

debt for you when He died on the Cross. "For the wages of sin is death, but the gift of God is eternal life in Jesus Christ our Lord" (Romans 6:23). God brought Jesus back from the dead. He provided the way for you to have a personal relationship with Him through Jesus. Trust Him. Pursue Him.

When we realize how deeply our sin grieves the heart of God and how desperately we need a Savior, we are ready to receive God's offer of salvation. To admit we are sinners means turning away from our sin and selfishness and turning to follow Jesus. The Bible word for this is "repentance"—to change our thinking to acknowledge how grievous sin is, so our thinking is in line with God's.

All that's left for you to do is to accept the gift that Jesus is holding out for you right now: "If you confess with your mouth, 'Jesus is Lord,' and believe in your heart that God raised him from the dead, you will be saved. For it is with your heart that you believe and are justified, and it is with your mouth that you confess and are saved" (Romans 10:9–10). God says that if you believe in His son, Jesus, you can live forever with Him in glory: "For God so loved the world that He gave his one and only Son, that whoever believes in him shall not perish, but have eternal life" (John 3:16).

Are you ready to accept the gift of eternal life that Jesus is offering you right now? Let's review what this commitment involves:

- I acknowledge I am a sinner in need of a Savior. I repent or turn away from my sin.
- I believe in my heart that God raised Jesus from the dead. I trust that Jesus paid the full penalty for my sins.
- I confess Jesus as my Lord and my God. I surrender control of my life to Jesus.

- I trust Jesus as my Savior forever. I accept that God has done for me what I could never do for myself when He forgives my sins.

If it is your sincere desire to receive Jesus into your heart as your personal Lord and Savior, then talk to God from your heart. Here's a suggested prayer:

> *Lord Jesus, I know that I am a sinner and I do not deserve eternal life. But, I believe You died and rose from the grave to make me a new creation and to prepare me to dwell in your presence forever. Jesus, come into my life, take control of my life, forgive my sins and save me. I am now placing my trust in You alone for my salvation and I accept your free gift of eternal life.*

If you've prayed this prayer, it's important that you take these three next steps: First, go tell another Christian! Second, get plugged into a local church. Third, begin reading your Bible every day (we suggest starting with the book of John). Welcome to God's forever family!

Made in the USA
Middletown, DE
23 April 2024